SPOT

FEELINGS

CONFUSED

by Rachel Bach

look up

scratch head

Look for these words and pictures as you read.

hand on chin

shrug

hand on chin

Damian feels confused.
He thinks hard.
He puts his hand on his chin.

shrug

Ali is puzzled.

She does not know the answer.

She shrugs.

scratch head

Eva's dad used a big word.

She does not know what he means.

She scratches her head.

It is okay to be confused.
You can ask questions.

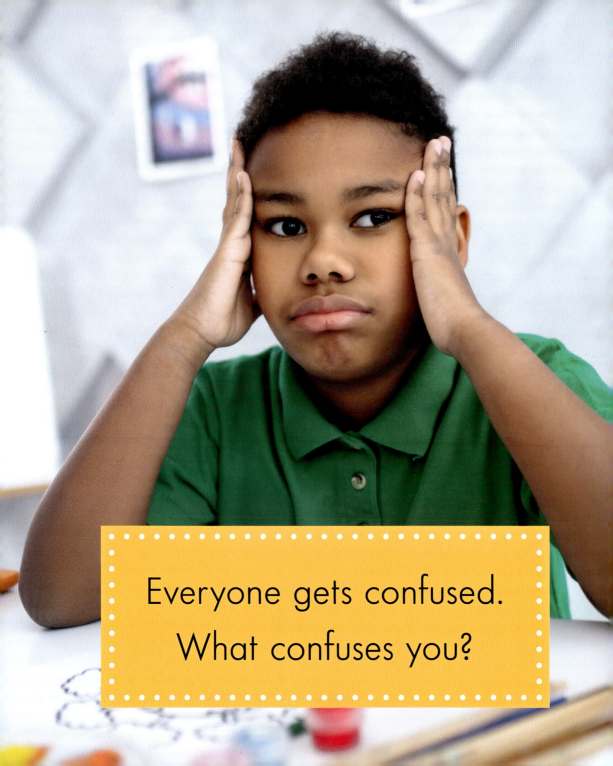

look up

scratch head

Did you find?

hand on chin

shrug

Spot is published by Amicus Learning, an imprint of Amicus
P.O. Box 227, Mankato, MN 56002
www.amicuspublishing.us

Copyright © 2025 Amicus.
International copyright reserved in all countries.
No part of this book may be reproduced in any form
without written permission from the publisher.

Library of Congress Cataloging-in-Publication Data
Names: Bach, Rachel, author.
Title: Confused / by Rachel Bach.
Description: Mankato, MN : Amicus Learning, [2025] |
   Series: Spot feelings | Audience: Ages 4–7 | Audience:
   Grades K-1 | Summary: "What makes kids feel
   confused? Encourage social-emotional learning with
   this beginning reader that introduces vocabulary for
   discussing feelings of confusion with an engaging
   search-and-find feature"– Provided by publisher.
Identifiers: LCCN 2024017567 (print) | LCCN 2024017568
   (ebook) | ISBN 9798892000796 (library binding) |
   ISBN 9798892001373 (paperback) |
   ISBN 9798892001953 (ebook)
Subjects: LCSH: Uncertainty–Juvenile literature. | Thought
   and thinking–Juvenile literature.
Classification: LCC BF463.U5 B33 2025 (print) | LCC
   BF463.U5 (ebook) | DDC 153.4–dc23/eng/20240503
LC record available at https://lccn.loc.gov/2024017567
LC ebook record available at https://lccn.loc.gov/2

Printed in China

Ana Brauer, editor
Deb Miner, series designer
Kim Pfeffer, book designer
and photo researcher

Photos by Dreamstime/Iryna
Tolmachova, 10–11, Yuri Arcurs, 4–5;
freepik/freepik, 12–13, zinkevych,
14; Getty Images/selimaksan, cover;
Shutterstock/aleks333, 8–9, Kues, 1, Luis
Molinero, 10, Roman Samborskyi, 3, SB
Arts Media, 6–7

CONFUSED